The Art of Networking

Your networking guide to success!

The Art of Networking

Practical & Easy • Tools & Strategies
Promote Yourself • Grow your Business

By Jennifer Harwood

Published by Jen Harwood Pty Ltd

ABN 27 086 387 288

PO Box 6137, White Hills, VIC 3550, Australia

Email: jen@jenharwood.com

Web: www.jenharwood.com

First printed January 2007
Second printing October 2009
Third printing May 2010

ISBN: 0-9802811-0-5

Cover design:	Craig Dunn, Filthy Monkey Productions www.filthymonkey.com.au
Graphic design:	Dale Harris, Studio Ink www.studioink.com.au
Copy Editing:	Gerri Kissner
Illustrator:	Grant Brown, Highly Tooned Creations www.tooned.com.au
Typset:	Jodie Bajada, BMP - Total Image Management www.bmp.com.au
Printer:	BMP - Total Image Management, Bendigo, Australia www.bmp.com.au

Acknowledgements

This book would not have been possible without the assistance of several people. Firstly, my parents...

My mother Cath, for teaching me at a very young age the power of intention, to always believe in self and others and always find the positive angle. My father Bob, for teaching me to never give up, to stand for what I believed in and to trust my instincts. --- My parents' success in life, family, marriage, relationships and their contribution to community have been through the principles in this book and.... they did it naturally. Thank you both for my life and teaching me the values and principles I can use to make a difference to others.

My sincere thanks to Gerri Kissner and Susie Forbes, both accomplished business consultants and professionals. Over the years both Gerri and Susie have given me support and encouragement to build my company, create opportunities and see a broader and wider picture than I thought was possible. Their unquestioning faith, trust and belief in me, even when I had moments of doubt, have been just awesome. Both Gerri and Susie are living examples of life long friendship, inspiration, teamwork and success.

I am very grateful to the National Speakers Association of Australia (NSAA) as this book was made possible by the Kerrie Nairn Scholarship[1] that I was awarded in 2006. The Scholarship gave me the confidence and strategy to produce a book and other products from my speaking efforts. The NSAA is an amazing organisation that is committed to growing and developing Australia's leading motivators, speakers, trainers and educators. I am proud to be a member of this organisation and encourage all readers of this book to consider becoming a speaker and sharing your message with the world!

Finally, my thanks to Robyn Faber. Robyn saw me deliver my first "Attraction in Action" presentation to a small 'Women in Business' breakfast in 2001 in Sydney, Australia. Robyn could see my potential and created opportunities for me to share my networking success and business building skills with others through events, forums and industry briefings. She always goes beyond her job role and responsibilities to create opportunities for all the businesses and people she meets. Robyn is a true networker and I am truly grateful for her encouragement, friendship and wisdom.

---

1   The Kerrie Nairn Scholarship is supported by the Australian Government through the Quality Outcomes Programme, administered by the Department of Education, Science and Training. Disclaimer: The views expressed do not necessarily represent the views of the Australian Government Department of Education, Science and Training."

A few words from Jennifer

Success is a funny thing. Over the years, I've read many goal setting, 'how to have a successful life' and business books. I've also attended numerous seminars, workshops and personal development programs and they all say basically the same thing...

Your success depends on YOU. You must be focussed, be persistent / determined / unstoppable and work hard. When I started my business in 1999, I took this on board and I did all of these things and after the first few years I reflected on my results and realised that while the results were good, I wasn't happy with them.

Yes, I'd focussed, worked hard and was unstoppable. The results I had were:

- I had very good sales, however they were always dependent on me creating new sales...there was no long term repeat business.

- I had equipment and infrastructure in the business, yet it was not being leveraged very well at all.

- I had people 'helping me out', yet the majority of 'help' was very short term and unreliable.

- I had a 7 year marriage that ended. All the effort of focussing on the business and 'getting results' had a heavy price in my personal life.

- I was frustrated, tired, angry and sad that all my focussed effort and hard work was... not working for me!

So, I had a deep hard look at what I was doing and finally realised what it was... I was doing everything BY MYSELF and doing it so hard that my whole life was suffering!!

The impact of doing everything by myself meant:

- I worked very, very long hours on my work & projects

- I wouldn't trust anyone with particular tasks or projects

- I wouldn't talk to anyone about what was going well or badly for the business or for me personally

- I would bottle up all my emotions about everything and detach

- My body and health were not in the best shape

- People around me felt that they couldn't connect with me personally

- My friends and family wouldn't call me because I was 'too busy'

- I didn't go out and have fun or play because everything was so serious all the time and I needed to be FOCUSSED on my goals. Sales and results fluctuated on my emotions, energy levels and attitude.

I was working hard and I didn't like it and the people around me didn't either. Sound familiar?? Something had to change and I finally worked out what it was....

I realised that I needed to involve other people and pro-actively network.

What does that mean, pro-actively network? Just to give you a picture, there were people around me, all the time actually, wanting to be a part of what I was doing and be involved. However, I never really let others participate or share my journey. It was all about me and what I was doing. I felt I had to work hard to get the results and sharing with others was a sign of weakness. I felt that I had to do it all on my own to deserve the results and the success. This is SO NOT TRUE.

Proactively networking is about sharing yourself, goals and dreams with others and they do the same with you. You focus on helping others realise their dreams and goals and they focus on doing the same for you. It's not just about business card swapping, quick hello handshakes and introductions. It's about creating value, being genuine and it's about wanting the best for others.

Networking is definitely the secret to business and personal success.

So, I've redefined success into the following formula:

Success = Focus + Being Unstoppable + Networking

Net-work instead of Hard-work !

Group action vs Individual action

Networking replaces the work hard factor.
Notice the word 'work' is still in the word 'networking'

HARD WORK	NETWORKING
Work hard by yourself	A big 'net' of people working

We now are living in a very fast paced world and technology such as email, media, computers and machines are assisting us to keep up the pace. However, at the end of the day, human connection and sharing is still THE MOST powerful way to create anything you want in any area of your business and life.

Most people these days are not taught how to pro-actively network and as such many miss out on wonderful opportunities and experiences because they are not sure how to use this amazing resource. This book is for all the business owners and people in the world that have been doing it HARD ON THEIR OWN, trying to make their world, or the world at large, a better place and only getting average results.

I encourage you, dear reader to partner with me in the ideas, strategies and tools in this book and start to build your networks, support teams and trusted people around you so that your growing 'NET' of people do more of the 'WORK' for you and that you become part of their networks of success !

Keep this book handy - in your bag, office, glove box or on your coffee table and refer to it often.

If you choose to do this, I promise, your results will be better, your life will be easier and your experience of work and building relationships will be uplifted, more than it has ever has been before.

I wish you a happy, rich and rewarding life working with others.

Jennifer

This book is dedicated to the most powerful and
resilient network I have - my family.

To my parents Bob & Cath, my grandmother Polly and my siblings Kate, Peter &
Brad (and their families): You all make my life rich with love, joy and happiness.
I am so proud to be a part of the Harwood Family.

Table of contents

HOW A NETWORK WORKS

What is a network?

A network is where a group of people get together to do one or more of the following:

- share and learn information and knowledge
- meet new people
- hear someone else speak
- get inspiration and confidence
- conduct business
- find resources, sales or leads
- share a passion or common interest, a sport, a belief or a hobby
- explore and experience life.

Networks are all about people connecting. Always remember this when you are networking: people want to sense a connection, feel normal and know there are others like them who are getting results. This is true for business associations, mothers' clubs, church groups, sporting groups, political groups, hobby and Special Interests Groups (SIGs).

You need to remember that the people in a network may be very different. They may come from all walks of life and socio-economic backgrounds. What they share however are common values and interests.

When you are choosing a network to participate in, it is best that you know the following about yourself before you approach a network:

1. Understand what your values are

2. Intention – know what you're looking to gain from a network

3. Intention - know what you are prepared to give to the network

Take a moment now, and list your top 5 Values.

Your values are what you deem important to you. If you are not sure about what your values are, take a moment now and look at your life. What are the top 5 things/key areas in your life that you MUST have.

For example, values that influence the people and places you network are:

Health • Car • Spouse • Children • Family • Money • House • Business • Friends • Holidays • Charity • Community • Invention • Creativity • Beauty • Peace • Love • Fishing • Football • Hobbies • Travel etc.

Your values

What are your top values? List out a few below before you choose the top 5

Your intention

What do you want from a network?

e.g. Sales, connections, fun, ideas
Confidence, time out from work
Learn new things, a night out!

What you want

_____

_____

_____

_____

_____

_____

_____

What are you willing to give?

e.g. Full participation, my skills
My contacts & connections
Leadership, take a committee role

What you will give

_____

_____

_____

_____

_____

_____

_____

> Be yourself and don't try to be what you think people want you to be. Remember, You are fabulous – so be yourself and share that. If you share common values with the group, you'll know very quickly whether you can support a network and if the network can support you.

Formal networks

Formal networks are organised, openly promoted and advertise for members to be part of the network. They are designed to link people, create opportunities, provide information and share resources. People come to these networks for all of these things in varying degrees. Many formal networks have a committee or a board that governs them, as well as key people responsible for membership, events and professional development.

Formal networks have events where many of their members attend. This provides excellent opportunity for you to meet new people and find people that you may have been wanting to connect with.

Joining formal networks usually involves membership fees. I encourage people to join a formal network as long as they can see value. If you are not sure, go along to several events to determine if you feel it will be of benefit.

Results from formal networks can be linked back to connections in the network and even specific events, activities or initiatives the network has created for individuals and the group. Many business people want to be able to measure their return on investment (time and money) from participating in a formal network.

Formal network example

In Nov 2004, I relocated my company from Mosman, Sydney, NSW to Bendigo, Victoria. I had chosen to make Bendigo my home town for family reasons and when I made the move, I did not know anyone in the Bendigo business community. Bendigo is a beautiful Australian country town and has about 100,000 people population. I also did not have a social network of friends as I had never lived in Bendigo before.

I was very nervous about the move on that level and knew the only way to make this really work was to get out of the office and the house and network! I knew my business and the work I did would speak for themselves!

That's exactly what I did. I started talking to the business people I was buying services and product from such as the local newsagent, local bottled water delivery man, the sign writer, mechanic and of course the local hairdresser! I found through my conversations with these wonderful people that Bendigo has a thriving business network called the Central Victorian Business Network (CVBN) and that is where I needed to go.

Within 3 weeks of moving to Bendigo, I attended the CVBN Dinner as the guest of my company sign writer, Peter Reading from Sign-A-Rama. There were 350 people at this event (which is normal for the CVBN) and the guest speaker talked about marketing and branding. All up I met about 35 people including one of the local businesswomen, Lilly Miszewski. I had met with Lilly a week prior to the dinner and she made sure she introduced me to local key people saying "you simply must meet Jennifer".

The results that came from that dinner, regular attendance at the CVBN events and follow up with people that I met in the first 12 months were:

Business Related Results

- Secured 20 new clients
- Referred countless people to each other and promoted others' businesses
- Developed a new product and sold it into the network
- I found businesses and services that my company needed and built relationships with the owners.
- I launched my professional speaking career and presented at 15 events as either the Keynote Speaker or as the MC.
- Was awarded Networker of the Month by the CVBN at one of the member dinners! (Yes, I had achieved my mission in 12 months).

Personal Related Results

- I established a great group of friends in the community
- I was inspired and learned from the people I met at events
- I learned from the keynote speakers at the events
- I had fun and really enjoyed myself

As you can see, the return on investment of my time (4 events per year) and membership fee (under $300) was definitely worth it.

What formal networks are around you?

List all the formal networks – even if you have not yet been to any events.

_____

_____

_____

_____

_____

Informal networks

Informal Networks have less organised structure than formal networks. People get involved with an informal network through conversation, referral and introduction. This type of network meets in smaller groups, usually from 2 - 10 people. An informal network's focus is about the people in it rather than the collective group. Their common value is that they are the same in some way.

Informal networks are usually driven by a person or group of people that are passionate about something. Their prime purpose is usually to help people in similar situations share information and/or inspiration. Many times, informal networks become more organised and then become formal networks. For example, my parents formed an informal network in Bendigo called the Bendigo Cancer Support Group. This group is for people with any type of cancer to come and share, listen and support others experiencing cancer.

The group started with a handful of people and met the third Tuesday of every month. There is no formal membership, fees, meeting agendas, roles or responsibilities of people in the group. It is passionately run by my parents and all they do is book a room at the local club and start the meeting's conversation and it runs from there.

This informal network has the potential to becoming a formal network. If it were to be formalised, it would need funding, some form of part-time or casual administrator and planning for the year. However at the moment it's serving the people that attend, very well and suits their needs, values and intentions, so at present it does not need to change.

Where do you find informal networks?

Create a list of everyone you know - either through your work or personally or both. You will be surprised who is on that list and how many people you actually know. Now, what is the common factor all of these people have? The common factor is that they know YOU.

This is your informal network. Now, I know you don't meet with everyone on your list every day, or some of them at all. That's OK.

Have a think about who you DO meet with on a regular basis? Regular could be weekly, fortnightly, monthly, yearly. The people you have chats with, meet after work, after an event or social function, meet for an extended period of time, or regularly meet down the pub on a Friday night. These meetings are your informal networks. You may just like the people you meet with socially and want to spend more time with them, or want to talk about politics or discuss events happening in your business environment. Whatever the reason and topic of conversation, this is an informal network.

The results from informal networks are harder to track. They can, however, be even more beneficial to the individual participants and the community. Don't underestimate the power of informal networks, especially when you want to make something happen quickly. Talking to people in an informal way about what you are doing and what you want, can quickly build support and momentum.

Informal networks - who do you know?

_____

_____

_____

_____

_____

5 keys to joining networks

From my experience, this is what works to enhance the connection when joining a network.

1. Buy local, preferably within the network. This helps you build rapport and relationships with the people in the network

2. Participate in network and related activities and events. This ensures that you build relationships and connections

3. Contribute to the network – give time, resources and skills, where appropriate

4. Keep a balance in your participation and do not over commit your time or resources. If you get out of balance, it won't work for you or the members in the network

5. Have fun and learn as you go. Your confidence will grow and your skills improve every time you participate.

Chapter 2

WHERE TO FIND A NETWORK

The Local Spot

Family

Friends

Email and news groups or newsletters

Buying or purchasing groups

Industry associations

Sports networks

Education networks

Community groups

Formal networks advertise and promote themselves. By reading the local paper and talking to local business people you can quickly identify where the local business networks are and when they meet.

Every city and most Australian towns have a chamber of commerce, several industry associations, employer associations and industry bodies. Government departments and their staff are a huge network to tap into. The key with government staff is to keep going until you find people that you 'click' with and can work with. Like anything, you've got to find like minded people.

Most cities in the world have professional community service groups such as Rotary, Lions, YsMen, APEX, Junior Chamber just to mention a few. In Australia, these services groups usually have their contact details on a sign somewhere on the way into a country town or near the town hall. If you are city based, look up your local group in the phone book or on the internet.

Informal networks such as mothers' clubs, self-help groups, dance groups, dating groups, cancer support groups etc are usually listed in the local paper. They may also provide fliers and brochures in local council chamber offices, sporting complex bulletin boards, doctors' surgeries, hospitals and supermarket notice boards.

There are many other ways of finding networks that may not be quite so obvious. I will outline the following:

- The Local Spot
- Family & Friends
- Email, Newsgroups, Blogs
- Buying Groups
- Industry Associations
- Sport, Education & Community Groups.

The Local Spot

The Local Spot is a fabulous way to network. The Local Spot is a place where people go to do something specific and is conducive to people meeting, talking and networking. Local spots include and are not limited to: the coffee shop, hairdresser/barber, the local gym, golf course, supermarket, child-care facility, park, shopping centre, video store. These places create networking opportunities as people are usually waiting around or coming to meet others to do something... ie. have coffee, workout, play golf, buy food. When people wait they usually notice other people and start conversations.

If you want to meet more people or catch up with someone you've only met once through business meetings, work out where they have lunch, coffee or play golf. When you know, go and be in those spots.

Now you don't want to be lurking there waiting just for them, that's called stalking! What you want to do is organise to meet your clients and friends at the chosen locations and wait to be seen by the people you want to meet. They will come up to you and say hello, or you could do the same. It's about being seen in the local spot and building on a conversation from there.

If you do connect with your target person (and sometimes you won't), remember that they didn't plan to meet you and you don't want to take up their time. Organise a time to meet them later. Local Spot networking is light, easy and simple. There's nothing heavy or serious about it as the local spot is fun and usually not work related.

The intention of local spot networking is... to be seen!

Family

Whether they are close to you or not, the people in your family are connected to you and share a common value with you. Family! - irrespective of similarities, differences, quarrels and general 'family stuff' that happens from time to time, your relatives generally want you to be happy. They know you better than anyone else and can help you to see yourself.

Most of us don't ask our family what they see, what they know and even who they know. If this is you, stop it right now, as you are missing a golden opportunity. The family perspective is important for all aspects of networking. For example, a member of your family may know a wealthy business person, knowledgeable community leader, a priest, lawyer, banker, medical specialist, healer who can help you, or someone who has been through what you are experiencing in life (birth, death, illness, winning the lottery!).

Whatever your need, your family should be your first point of call. Why? Well, if they can't help you initially, they will be on the look-out on your behalf, long after mere acquaintances forget your request for help.

The best way to support your family network is to participate 100% in it. Yes, get involved with family activities - don't just show up, be interested in them. For some people that may be tough. I promise you - it's worth it. Get over yourself and any minor disagreements or major grudges and want the best for each member of your family. Find out one small thing that's important to each family member and then set to work on delivering that. Don't make a big song and dance about what you're doing – just quietly do it for them. Your support for their need, or want, will help them and they will want to do the same for you. Invest in your family!

The intention of Family networking is...want for them what they want and help them get it!

Friends

Like your family, your friends want you to be happy. Your friends share many values with you and not all of your friends share the same values as one another. The common factor between your friends is YOU. The key to growing your network of friends is sharing yourself and staying in contact.

Share what's going on, the good and the bad. Keep it real and drama/saga free. Your friends love you and love being part of your life. Keep them involved in your activities by talking to them and keeping in contact.

Some friends won't stay around for your whole life, as both of your values and priorities will shift over time. That's OK. You want to create a network of true friends that is broad in culture, age, experience and is as fulfilling to them as it is to you. The other key to your friends' and family networks is to ask for assistance when you really need it. Your friends, like your family, are connected to a whole variety of people you don't even know.

While you don't want to be always needing assistance and leaning on your family and friends so that you create a burden, you don't want to be an island and distant from everyone - it's about BALANCE. You want your friends to know that they can count on you to be there for them and that they will be there for you. Friends and family are the informal, long-term networks that, if viewed as a lifetime investment, can be the greatest asset you ever have.

The intention of Friend networking is...share yourself and let them share with you. Don't try to 'fix' your friends.

Email and news groups or newsletters

People in these groups share the value of pooling information about a common subject. In some cases they support a network that meets regularly and they publish pictures of the events, as the members of the network value recognition. News groups mostly network online and share information and experiences. Online networks are a lot less personal and you need to check the information you get. This type of network can open many doors, stimulate thinking and create connection contacts way outside of your local area, as they usually operate globally. What online groups or newsletters could support you and your endeavours?

Buying or purchasing groups

The common value here is money – making it and saving it! One example is an industry association that buys an insurance policy to cover all members. Members then subscribe to be part of the association to gain substantially discounted insurance premiums. Another opportunity is a cooperative that buys or sells local produce to a bigger market to create better, more regular, reliable prices for the primary growers. These networks also share the common value of group purchase and collective power. They are very useful for the smaller business or person to get involved with in order to save money and network with likeminded people. What buying groups could you and/or your business be a part of?

Industry associations

There are thousands of industries and therefore thousands of industry associations. That's great news, as there's likely to be an association for what you are looking for – whether it's a manufacturing association or a business services association or to have some fun, the People Living with Cats Association. The common value in associations is generally the value of the activity the association stands for. The key to this type of network is that you do what the association members do or are connected to it in some way. You need to have relevance to participate in this type of network. For example, if you want to join the People Living with Cats Association, you will need to own a cat and/or live with a cat or run a business that sells cat products!

Industry associations have a specific conversation, their own jargon, and they like it that way. In fact, an industry association loves that they can talk to each other "in their own language" as they usually can't anywhere else in their lives.

Let me give you an example of this:

- Imagine attending a medico-legal conference and you are not a doctor or a lawyer?

- Imagine attending an informal discussion with a room full of mothers discussing the different experiences they had when they were giving birth when you have never had a baby or been to a birth?

- Imagine attending a furniture industry annual dinner where the guest speaker talks about the specifics of chair manufacture, production and types of wood and how they respond to the outside daily temperature when all your experience about chairs has been sitting on them!

I have been to network events in these situations and more and let me tell you, each association's language and jargon work for them – being able to talk together in detail about their particular area of knowledge is one of their shared values – and it's up to YOU to get your head around it if you want to participate. Make sure you do not complain, berate or put down the association or people in it. Keep your opinions about them and the association at home.

Be open to learning, listening and being patient. As you get to learn the language and start to appreciate the association's way of communicating, momentum builds and networking gets easier. It helps to have a friend who's "in the know" about the industry and willing to teach you a few of the key pieces of jargon; they will be able to introduce you to others.

The key to success with industry associations is not to be put off by the first few meetings or events. Give yourself a goal to participate 100% and review after six months. People in this type of network will appreciate your commitment and assist you the more you attend and participate.

Blogs and online

Blogs are a rapidly growing phenomenon and should not be overlooked in networking. They are yet another totally new way of communicating with a wide variety of people who you may or may not connect with. Blogs provide an insight into another's life – sometimes there may be too much information – however, it is another form of connecting to others and they to you. Remember though, blogs and online communication can be the starting point of networking or, over time, enhance networking and build the relationship.

So, my advice with Blogs and online media is, when you network, balance online connection with real life. Relying on just one may cost you opportunities.

Sports networks

People in a sporting network have a common value, the love of the game. There are networks for people who play the sport, watch the sport – and even networks for people who collect memorabilia from a sport. Depending on the level of knowledge about the sport in the network, there will be an equivalent level of sporting jargon. Again, the key to this type of network is relevance and an understanding of the game; or if you don't understand, a keen willingness to learn about the sport.

For example, you need to know the main teams and players and the weekly scores. Do your homework away from the network by reading the newspapers, watching the games on TV and learn more about the sport including some history; or if you're playing the game, refine your skills and knowledge with a sporting coach.

Education networks

Everyone has been to school and more often than not these days, people are doing some form of further education. The people you meet in an education and learning environment can be great for networking – you tend to build closer relationships with them as you are regularly going to class once or twice a week for a period of time. The key to education networks is to participate. You benefit as you get the learning from the education program you are in, as well as building connections with people in the class. Share your contact information with others and keep in touch if that is relevant to you.

Community groups

Community groups are very powerful networks. The smaller the community, the greater the strength. A new person to the network doesn't usually see this, as a small community has many members wearing different hats, acting in different roles to make the network/community function.

Small country towns have this networking quality – they don't exclude others on purpose, it's simply a function of how a network survives. Those who commit to the network want to ensure its growth so they then benefit from their participation.

The key to participating in community groups and networks is to appreciate the values of the network and be a part of it. Be patient and participate with the group, don't try to put your stamp on everything. Communities are a reflection of the Whole Group, not just one individual, so your continual participation will make your community great and you will receive the benefits of being a part of it.

Be yourself...and genuinely interested in the people in the community.

Think and act with a long term perspective.

7 steps to start networking

1. Know what you want and the type of people you want to meet.

2. Identify all your options of networks BEFORE joining any.

3. Pick one network to participate in. (No more than 2 networks to start with).You will get faster results as well as optimise your time and energy, if you focus on up to 2 networks rather than going to every event, meeting and networking group that exists.

4. Get involved and give your full effort and participation.

5. Don't big note yourself, brag, gossip or complain about anything until you know the group/network better. Then when you know the network better, get on the leadership team and just change the things that don't work.

6. Follow up after the event with each person you met.

7. Be yourself at all times and learn the language of the network of which you want to be a part.

Chapter 3

NETWORKING ETIQUETTE

Be appropriate

Be consistent

Watch your language

Make requests clear & easy

Manage your 'day drama'

Understanding networking etiquette is essential to being successful at it. Most of it is just common sense and some is an unspoken code of conduct. The keys are:

Be appropriate

The way you present yourself must be appropriate for the event and the type of people you are meeting. This does two things for you:

- It gives you credibility within the group
- It removes any distractions for the people you are talking to

Your appearance must reinforce your credibility – first impressions last.

My point here is that you must be relevant and appropriate. It's OK to wear your company polo shirt to business events if you sell pools, spas, do lawns, sell security and have a company uniform. You don't always have to wear a suit. If the event is smart casual, you still need to look neat.

Be authentic

You have to be yourself. Don't try to pretend to be anything other than yourself. If you try to turn yourself into something you think people want you to be, they will see that you are being fake. If you are shy, be shy. If you are outspoken, be outspoken, if you are smart and savvy, don't be an idiot ! When you network, people want to know who they are dealing with and who you are. The key to being authentic is to realise the impact you will have on other people and be responsible about it.

I went to a networking event in Sydney and a woman there was dressed in an elegant, brightly coloured outfit topped with a beautiful hat. She looked amazing and while she didn't conform to the event's dress code, she was appropriate as she makes and sells designer hats! I was so curious about her business that I went to her shop and there were gorgeous hats everywhere. Her business thrives on special occasions and the Melbourne Cup. She had worked out that her best way to market her business was to wear the product and she did it in a way that was appropriate to the business events she went to.

Be consistent

The other factor with clothes is when you go away from home on a business trip, conference or on a holiday. What clothes should you pack?

My general tip is that everyone (men and women) should pack both formal and casual for every trip. The proportion of formal and casual clothes will depend on your trip. If you are going on holidays to the beach for 2 weeks, at the bottom of your bag have a complete formal outfit - just incase you need to have a business meeting or go out with someone special!

Similarly, if you are going on a business trip, you need to have some casual gear. You may go out for dinner, lunch or relax by the pool. You don't necessarily want to be doing that in your business attire. A word of warning, make sure your casual dress reflects your work.

> I was at a business conference where the conference delegates wore suits. An informal group activity of a pool party was organised where spouses were invited to attend.
>
> One conference delegate wore a shirt that had offensive language on it. She thought it was great, I could tell from her body language she was very proud of her shirt and was very comfortable in it. However, I noticed that other people were offended by the shirt and made a judgment about who this woman was and if they were going to talk to her.

If you are going to wear clothing with a message on it, make sure it's appropriate and you are prepared for the impact it will create.

Watch your language

Even if you look the part, your use of language and words could let you down. Refrain from swearing, even if others do. Listen to the language of many of the people in the network – check how you are talking and the words you are using and make sure you match.

Never compromise your own values and principles. If people are using the kind of language that you're not comfortable with, rethink your choice to be involved with that network.

Manage your behaviour

Be consistent with your actions. What you do outside the network, with friends, family, in the community and in your life generally, will be noticed by others. I encourage people to think about how they behave outside of work, what they do, where they go, and make it all consistent. Excessive drinking, smoking, swearing, substance abuse, over-working, destructive relationships, drama and poor health can impact your results in business and career.

Please know that I am not here to make judgments about people and what they do. At the end of the day it's your life and you must live it. If you are not getting the results you want at work or in business, take a look at how you are behaving in your personal life and see if you are consistent. If you are not consistent, change your behaviour. Similarly, if the people around you are experiencing the same results, it may be time to change your group of friends.

Be on time

Points to note:

- you need to show up a bit before the event is due to start. That's when the networking actually happens. Also, if you have a car that has signage on it, park it near the entrance to the event to get maximum exposure

- If you are late, come in quietly and don't announce you are late to everyone, except the host. Get in and start talking to people without going on about how and why you were late, it's not important to others.

Wear your name badge

Most networking events give you a name badge or sticker with your name on it. Wear it! Also, when you wear it, put it on your right lapel jacket so people can see your name. Most of the time when you shake hands to greet someone, they will shake your right hand, look you in the eye and then look down to your name badge.

I have seen people wear their name badge on their hip or on their glasses chain down in the middle of their chest, or under their coat! This doesn't work and doesn't make it easy for someone to see your name, and company. Remember also to ensure your name is easy to read - some people need glasses to read and may feel quite uncomfortable if your name is too small to see easily.

However, if you need glasses to read, you can use this to you're advantage!

When you meet someone new and have trouble reading their name badge, break the ice by playing up the fact you can't read without glasses - squint and peer closely and laugh when you ask their name. I have a friend who does this to her advantage. It is not only a novel way that she introduces herself and she is easily remembered. She is not faking it - just being who she is!!

Your name badge is not for you…
its for everyone else !

Food at events

Sit down dinners can be overwhelming if you are not confident about table etiquette. Don't panic, either get some tips before you go or take the lead from others at the table who appear to know what to do. There is a general rule: use the cutlery from the outside in for each course.

A smorgasbord can tempt you to pile the yummy food onto your plate. DON'T! Rather have smaller portions so you can go back to the smorgasbord and meet others. Just make sure you make 1-2 trips or you will add unwanted kilos all in the name of networking!!

Cocktail Events can be tricky where you battle to balance a glass and a plate of food. I have found that I can rest a small plate on top of my glass if I need to shake hands or exchange business cards. Just don't shake hands too hard and be sure you can hold it all together. If you're not confident, rather than a plate, use a serviette to hold finger food or put your glass down nearby until you have finished eating.

Also, whenever you are offered finger food take a serviette ALWAYS! You never know if you're going to need it - it's a great backup for spills and mouth wipes!

Wherever you are eating, don't stuff your mouth full or try to speak while eating. Remember you are there to meet and speak with other people and you don't want to lose the opportunity to connect with someone because you have a mouthful of food. Of course this can't always be avoided, however you can minimise the possibility of it occurring. If you are on the receiving end of this situation, make light of it and wait until the person has finished eating before starting a conversation. More than likely each one of us has been caught with a mouthful at the wrong time!

Wine/alcohol will probably be provided with your meal. If you prefer water, ask for it otherwise DO NOT DRINK TOO MUCH. In fact drink no more than one glass of wine to ensure you are in control of your behaviour and that you remember the conversation and those you are meeting. After all that is what you are there for!

For those of you who are like me and don't drink very often or at all, I have a simple way of avoiding the conversation about why I'm not drinking at an event. I ask for mineral water with lime in a wine glass. It's refreshing and 'looks' appropriate and no-one, except the waiter, knows.

Make requests clear & easy

There's nothing more frustrating than someone who beats around the bush, mumbles, makes excuses and apologises when asking for things. If you want something, ask for it clearly and directly. Don't confuse people.

For example:

- "I would like to talk with you more about your company's current needs. When would be a good time to do that?"

Rather than:

- "If it's not to much trouble to you… and I know this is short notice…do you think it would be OK if I called you next week to find out when you would be able to… I know you are busy… able to see me for about oh, say, 20 minutes or more? Would that be OK? It's OK to say no".

When you are direct and clear, there are three possible responses to any request:

1. Yes
2. No
3. A counter offer – the other person wants to accept your request, and has a different solution. Your job is to see if the counter offer works for you; if it does, accept it.

When you know these are the only three outcomes to a direct request, it makes it much easier to ask.

Manage your 'day drama'

We are all living our lives the best we can and we all have 'Day Drama' going on. This is all the stuff of life you're dealing with – your boss, your staff, sick children, your significant other, having a lot of pressure at work and you trying to create a serene environment at home, your parents are visiting for a month, you have a boss who's impossible to please and/or you have a staff member who's not performing, you're being audited, you've had a toothache all week and you can't see the dentist for another four days, you can't remember when you had a moment to get outside in the sun, read the paper or have 30 minutes of peace for lunch… get the picture?

When you have all that day drama in your head, how can you possibly listen to anyone else? Simply put, you CAN'T listen and be present for the other person.

Day drama is also a nightmare for the person hearing it. Have you ever been to an event where someone is telling you all the stuff of their day? It's usually negative, uninspiring, boring and not the type of conversation you came to the event to have. Be responsible and clear your head of day drama before you get to the event. The easiest way to do that is to find a quiet spot (in your car, or at your office before you leave for the event) and take a few minutes to look at the day drama in your head and stop it distracting you. Put it to the side, or mentally leave it in the car or at the office. It won't go anywhere if you don't want it to and you can always collect it when you get back!

NETWORKING TOOLS

Business cards

Business card essentials

Where to keep your business cards?

Business cards in your wallet

When do you give your card out?

What do you do with their card?

Two-pocket card manoeuvre

Brochures or products

Digital material

Website

Phone, mobile & email

Checking messages

Confidence

Databases

So now you have identified a network you want to be involved in and are aware of how to conduct yourself in the network, there are practical tools that can help you make the most of networking.

Business cards

A business card contains all your contact details and generally a message about who you are and what you do. It is a great tool for networking as it can start a conversation, complete a conversation or even enhance a conversation.

There are many questions I get about business cards - what to have on them, what to do with them and how to use them. Firstly, you need something to give to people that's easily read with all your contact details on it. So if you have not got one, go get some made up.

Business cards don't have to cost the earth – it is easy to make business cards yourself at home using your computer and some pre-cut stationery if you are just starting out. I encourage people to go get professional cards printed. For professional business cards I use www.businesscards.net.au and they provide quality cards to anywhere in Australia really fast.

Business card essentials

I have listed the information in order, for you to have on your business card, from the most important to the least. The first seven elements are essential.

1. Your name – make it easy to see

2. Your position or title – under your name

3. Your business name

4. Your business address

5. Your best contact phone number – mobile and/or work. This must be a number you will answer and check messages on regularly

6. Your email address

7. Print the card on thicker paper (100gsm)

---

8. Your business website

9. Your business logo

10. Your company image and colours

11. Your company slogan

12. On the back of the card, have three to four key points about what your company offers.

Some people will be horrified that the last five points are not essential to a business card. I understand, and to those of you on the floor needing resuscitation... relax.

The reason I believe that the first seven elements are essential is that I have spoken to hundreds of people over the years about why they do not network or enjoy networking. For most people, what stops them networking is the fact that they spend all of their time trying to finalise one of the last five elements in the list. For example, they need to get the logo finalised, the colours sorted out, the slogan or unique selling proposition (USP) clear or the website finished before they will start networking.

Too often, people are waiting to have the perfect business card, company logo, design and image BEFORE they network. This limits their confidence and prevents them from creating opportunities, getting out there and taking daily steps forward.

If you are reading this and have been agonising about your logo, your business colours, your website, the whole look and feel of your business card – stop that right now! It's not working for you!

Go and get some cards made with just the basics on them. I promise you, you will upgrade your cards very quickly as you get clear about what you're doing and the message you want to get across through networking and having conversations with other people.

If you wish, keep the back of the card blank with a matt finish so you can write any information for or about someone else.

One last word of advice – do not apologise for your card. Your card is the way it is and that's it. Even if your card is not perfect, you can work with it for now. So, if you accept your card as it is, others will too. No one likes to deal with fuss and apology over something that is nothing to do with them.

I was at a networking event as the keynote speaker. There were about 100 people there and I was presenting the Art of Networking. Now my business cards had the wrong phone number on it. I found out the morning of the event. I was devastated and didn't want to do the event because 'I'd look stupid because I couldn't even get my own card right!' What did I do? Nothing! That was the card I had and when I gave everyone my card at the event I told them to email me. The next day I fixed the card and ordered new ones that were correct!

Accept what you have and work with it.

Where to keep your business cards?

You want to have your cards with you everywhere. Keep some at home, in the glove box of your car, on your desk, in your bag or briefcase, in your spouse's car & bag/briefcase. You just never know when you will need a business card and it's best to have them stashed EVERYWHERE just in case!

I was in Circular Quay in Sydney on a hot Sunday afternoon. I was coming back from the beach and was not working. I was stuck in gridlock traffic and, not knowing when the traffic was going to move again, I started looking around at the people in their cars. The traffic going the other direction had stopped too. A man in a van smiled at me and I rolled down my window and said to him, 'So, what do you do?' He looked a bit surprised at the boldness of my question and then answered.

I replied, 'How's business going?'

He answered, 'It could be better, we need to grow our sales.'

At this point I said, 'Really, that's very interesting.'

He countered, 'Why, what do you do?'

I replied,' I help businesses grow by writing business plans, coaching business owners and generally get businesses moving!'

His answer was, 'Really, do you have a business card?'

I panicked for a minute - here was a golden opportunity to network and I didn't have a card. I didn't have my business card holder on me. Frustration was just about to kick in when I remembered I have a box of business cards in the glove box. So I pulled on the handbrake, stretched over, opened the glove box and pulled out a business card. I held it up and smiled.

He said, 'Throw it to me.' I did, he caught it and then, quick as a flash, the traffic started to move, I released the handbrake and we both drove off in different directions. I didn't even know what his name was.

The next day at my office I got a call from the man in the van about his business. We met later that week and my company ended up doing a significant amount of work with his business.

Business cards in your wallet

Guys, this one is particularly for you. Do not keep a wad of business cards in your wallet. The number of men I see with a big fat wallet in their back pocket with business cards… and everything else in their life in it… Really, it doesn't work !!

I suggest that everyone (men and women) only keep three business cards in your wallet/purse for emergencies. Have you ever seen someone hunting through their wallet and purse looking for their card and you can see how much money they have, how many receipts, credit cards and pictures of their loved ones? People will make assumptions about you about what they see/don't see in your wallet/purse.

A business card holder is the best option. They come in leather, metal and many people have designer cases or company cases. Pick a style that works for you. Your cards are for business purposes and they need to be kept in something that will keep them fresh, clean and ready to be received.

The business card holder can be for men, kept in their lapel jacket pocket, their top shirt pocket or even their back pant pocket. For women, the business card holder can be kept again in suit pockets or in a handbag with easy access.

When do you give your card out?

You give your business card to someone when they ASK FOR IT. When you meet someone new, don't just thrust a card at them – they didn't invite you to do that. Remember, your job when networking is to be interested in the other person and create interest for them in what you do and how you can be of service to them.

If they want to know more, they will ask you for your card. When they do, give it to them and then you can then ask them for their card.

What do you do with their card?

Look at it – don't just grab it and put it in your pocket, business card holder or bag straight away. Your 'look' at the card should last as long as it takes to count to three in your head. Looking at the card this way does a number of things for you:

- It helps you later when you look at the card to connect to the person, what they looked like and what they said.

- Business cards, a lot of the time, reflect the person. Who they are is on the card – looking at it with the person present shows them respect and that you are interested in them.

- It also gives you the opportunity to get more information about the person that they might not have mentioned already.

- It gives you something else to talk about. This might be no more than 'Oh, you live in Perth. How long have you been there?' This shows the other person you're interested and it keeps you both talking.

- If your business markets itself via email and the person's email address is on the card, you can say something like, 'We have a newsletter, would you like me to send it to you?' If they answer yes, you have permission to email them, and you can note that on their card later.

When you have looked at the card, put it somewhere safe. Many people get confused with giving and receiving cards and they end up giving other people's cards out, not their own!

Two-pocket card manoeuvre

When I network, I aim to wear a jacket with two pockets. The right side has my cards in it and the left is for other people's cards. When I don't have pockets I use my business card holder, which has two sides to it. One side has my cards and the other is for other's cards.

Have a system for giving and receiving cards that works for you.

Brochures or products

If you are networking to promote a product or your company and there's more to
it than a three-minute description, have a brochure of the product/service (or a
sample of the product if it's not too big and cumbersome) with you in your bag.

A word of warning – only show brochures or products to people who are really
interested. You'll know they are interested as they will have asked you insightful
questions and are genuinely interested. Only when you have that type of
conversation is when you give them a brochure or show them the product.

There are two reasons for doing this:

*   You don't want to be rude and shove, what you think is brilliant, at a person
    you've just met who is not really interested

*   Giving samples of products and brochures to people who are not interested
    costs you money and time.

Digital material

Any digital material such as CDs or DVDs is great for carrying further information.
Most people will look at a CD or DVD to see more about you and the business
you represent when they get home or back at the office.

Again, only give CD/DVDs to people who are genuinely interested. Think carefully
about what information it incorporates – make sure it is relevant, interesting, and
will tell people what they need to know about your product/service and your
company.

Website

A website creates the opportunity for people you have met to find out more about
you and your company. It can fill in the gaps and enable them to find out more.

Your website doesn't need to be expensive to build or maintain, however it must
be easy to find, navigate and provide relevant information to the conversation you
would have had with the person you met. If you have a website make sure your
web address is on your business card.

Phone, mobile & email

Phone

Make it easy for people to contact you. Have a voice message that's positive, interesting and encourages people to leave a message themselves. Your voicemail message reinforces who you are to your listener. If you are generally a happy, fun, out going person and your message is dull and boring, the listener will get a mixed message as to who you are.

For example, the message on my phone is, "Hi, this is Jennifer. I'm not available at the moment so please leave your name number and message after the beep. Thanks for your call and remember, make today fantastic, it's never coming again! Bye."

Every message that's left for me is along the lines of…

"Hi Jennifer that's great, I'm having a fantastic day..." and then they leave me the message.

So why have an upbeat phone message? I do that that for two reasons.

1. My own self-interest – I want happy messages left on my voicemail.

2. My clients know me as being high energy and they like to get a dose of that enthusiasm when they ring me.

When recording your message on either your business or mobile phone, make sure you smile! If you can't get into smiling, try this trick.

Take a pen and push it horizontally between your teeth, (like a flamenco dancer with a rose). Push the pen back as far as you can so that the edges of your mouth are a bit stretched.

Go look at yourself in the mirror! You have created a smile, whether you like it or not! You'll feel really stupid doing this and you'll probably laugh at yourself anyway.

If that is not your style, play some happy music really loud and feel it, or read or tell a joke, find a friend to tickle your feet – whatever it takes, get happy before you record your message.

Mobile

Make sure your mobile doesn't have an annoying or unprofessional ring tone. Also choose a reliable model, with all the features you need and will use, rather than just the latest gimmicks.

Email

Your email address should reflect you and/or your business. For example, an email like sexygirl13@hotmail.com won't be appropriate unless you are in the business of intimate apparel!

Checking messages

You must check all your messages (email & phone) at least twice a day and call people back on the same day if possible. If you are going to be away for some time, make sure your voice messages and email systems are set up to notify people and provide an alternate contact for them in your absence.

Confidence

You can enhance your networking with psychological tools as well as physical ones. Networking is all about sharing yourself. Many people find this very challenging as they think they won't have anything to talk about, they don't want to say much about themselves etc.

The following exercise can prepare you, and give you confidence on subject areas and information about yourself that's not too personal.

Confidence list exercise

1.   List what you are good at (work or personal)

_____

_____

_____

_____

_____

2. List things you just love to do (work or personal)

_____

_____

_____

_____

_____

3. List topics that you know something about (work or personal)

_____

_____

_____

_____

_____

4. List experiences you have had (work, holidays, places) that you could say something about.

_____

_____

_____

_____

_____

5. List all the jobs you've ever had and what you did

_____

_____

_____

_____

_____

6. List your top 5 favourite Christmas or Holiday Events

_____

_____

_____

_____

_____

7. Write a list of your closest 25 friends. Then list next to their name three things that are interesting about them.

Friend   **What's intersting about them**

_____   _____

_____   _____

_____   _____

_____   _____

_____   _____

_____   _____

_____   _____

_____   _____

_____   _____

_____   _____

_____   _____

_____   _____

_____   _____

_____   _____

Continued over page

7. Write a list of your closest 25 friends. Then list next to their name three
    things that are interesting about them.

Friend   **What's intersting about them**

_____   _____

_____   _____

_____   _____

_____   _____

_____   _____

_____   _____

_____   _____

_____   _____

> **Remember - networking is about conversation. You don't have to
> drive the conversation, just participate. You do not need to be an
> expert in anything to newtork.**

When you have done this, you will see that you DO HAVE lots of things to talk
about. If you can't list anything for yourself (which I doubt is the case), your
backup is the list of 25 friends you made. They are interesting and I'm sure you
know a bit about their interests and could talk about that.

Databases

Great networkers can ALWAYS find the name of a
person to refer in almost every situation.

The final, most important took is keeping a sound database of all the people you
have met, done business with and referred. Ideally you want to be able to email
direct and keep track of your contact. My advice with databases:

1. Use a database that you know how to use. Some people buy elaborate
   database systems that they struggle and fight with, and this doesn't work.
   Simple databases, suct as ACT and even Microsoft Outlook, can be enough for
   many businesses

2. Regularly back it up and saved / stored off site

3. Keep important names and contacts easily accessible in your PDA or organiser

4. When you come back from a networking event, put the names and details
   of everyone you have met into your database. (Try to do it the same day not
   schedule to do it in a week's time, because you will never do it!)

5. Your database can also be great for remembering birthdays, names of your
   clients spouse, children and pets

6. Some databases have excellent customer relationship management systems
   built in so you can be reminded of follow up activity, meetings and actions
   to do

7. Make sure you identify what type of information you need to collect about
   your customers, sales and business processes before you invest in any
   technology or database software.

The more organised you are with contact
management, the more successful you
will be at networking.

Chapter 5

KEYS FOR SUCCESSFUL NETWORKING

Have an intention

The networking buddy

Centres of influence

Create the conversation thread

Alliances

Creative thinking

Momentum

Remember, networking events are places where initial impressions are made. If you are relevant, credible and appropriate, you don't have to do anything, make a deal, or collect 50 business cards to make an impact or be noticed. It's best to just be there and be yourself.

There are 7 particular keys that can create successful networking.

They are:

1. Have an intention
2. The networking buddy
3. Centres of influence
4. Create the conversation thread
5. Alliances
6. Creative thinking
7. Momentum.

1. Have an intention

Intentions are powerful for creating results when networking. Be clear about what you want and why you want it. You have chosen a particular networking group to participate in, so keep clear in your mind why you are there. Your intentions and reasons for being there are your own and whatever they are is fine.

Remember to check your intentions at the end of the event and see how you went. You'll be surprised how well you did. Make sure you congratulate yourself for taking action and wanting to grow beyond what you know. If you didn't achieve everything, on the way home think about what you could have done differently to create the result you wanted. Don't despair – practice makes perfect and sometimes we need to do a lot of practice to achieve our desired goals!

Examples of intentions

Overall intentions for joining the network:

- To be a participating member in a like-minded community
- To grow my business and generate business leads, opportunities and sales
- To share my knowledge and experience and help others
- To have more fun and laughs
- To get out of my regular routine and learn something new.

Event-specific intentions:

- Meet five new people today
- Create five new work opportunities for my business
- Listen to everyone intently
- Give at least five gems of my experience and information to anyone that asks me for my thoughts
- Check the time every 30 minutes to see if I'm having fun and if I am, smile; if I'm not, I'll create some
- Learn three new things tonight.

2. The Networking buddy

If you do go to a networking event on your own, a useful strategy to start meeting people is to find a person and make them your networking buddy for the event.

So, how you do that is:

1. Introduce yourself to someone you don't know

2. Talk to them, and if it seems appropriate with this person, suggest that you become networking buddies for the event

3. Explain to them that you want them to get the most out of this event and ask them what their intentions are

4. Then ask them about their business or work and make sure you know what they do and what they are hoping to achieve from the event

5. Share your intentions for the event and explain what it is that you do as well to them

6. Take 10 business cards of theirs and give 10 of yours so you can support each other when networking at the event

7. Agree to meet up halfway through the event or at a break to see how the other is doing with their intentions

8. At the end of the event, see if you both got what you came for. If you did, celebrate and if you didn't, acknowledge the achievement of coming and networking and think about what you can do differently next time. Practise makes perfect. Also remember you now know one more person in the network, your event buddy!

3. Centres of influence

Centres of influence are people that know a lot of other people, are connected to a great number of groups and can influence the conversation, discussion and make introductions.

A person that is a centre of influence can help you access other networks, facilitate introductions to key people and can endorse you to a network (if you prove competent to them in who you are and what you do).

These people are sometimes not always the people who make the most noise or are up at the front of a room. Many of them are background people who are involved in a lot of things – they get in and make it happen.

That's why they know a large number of people and have something that is very powerful – their word creates action and generates results. When you come into a network it is always a good idea to look for the people who are the centres of influence and observe them.

Understand who they are and what motivates them. Get to know them and, most of all, be yourself with them. Listen to what they say and take their advice or direction. Centre of influence people know more about what's going on in the network than you do. Don't waste their time if you're not prepared to take their advice. Don't gossip about them or say negative things that may affect their credibility. More often than not, if you do this you damage your own credibility very quickly.

4. The conversation thread

Conversation and communication are fundamental to networking. Speaking, listening and the words you use are so important. You need to be clear about the message you want to convey, so that when you do get the opportunity to speak to someone, the message you have is clear. Some people call it your elevator pitch or your Unique Selling Proposition. They are great things to have, however, what this is about is simple – what is it that you want people to remember about you or your message?

It is important that the message you want to convey is clear and replicable. For example:

Sally is at a networking event and she's just bought the local stationery business. The messages she wants to impart are:

1. The business is under new management and she's the new owner

2. Sally is an expert in stationery and has hired new staff that are business focused

3. The business is moving into office furniture as well.

Sally	"Hi Dave, I'm Sally Smith and I've just bought the local stationery store – Office National from Pete Jones."
Dave	"Hi Sally, wow that's impressive, I bet it's all new to you at the moment?"
Sally	"No actually, I own 3 stationery stores in other towns and have brought over into this business 2 very good staff who know how to talk to business people."
Dave	"That's great, I've been frustrated with the level of service from the previous staff."
Sally	"Say Dave, from the feedback and research I did before buying the Office National business, it seems to me that the area lacks a supply of affordable, good quality office furniture. Is that the case?"
Dave	"Yes it is, are you thinking of doing something about that?"
Sally	"Yes, we are able to supply office furniture to all the local businesses. I can have a catalogue delivered into your office tomorrow if you'd like."

Dave   "Wow, yes, that would be great."

Dave now speaks with Brian.

Dave   "Hey Brian, I just met Sally Smith. She's just moved to the area from Sydney and bought Pete's Office National business. She's got 3 other stationery stores already and is focusing on business solutions. Sally said she'll drop off an office furniture catalogue to my office tomorrow. How about that?"

Brian   "Office furniture! Great, where is she, I'd like to talk to her about a new filing cabinet as mine won't shut!"

If you are clear about the messages you want to leave with people, you will see results faster.

5. Alliances

Alliances are people that support & believe in you and you in turn support and believe in them.

Having people you know gives you courage and strength to speak up, take risks and create momentum. Most people don't go to a networking or even a social event by themselves, as it takes a lot of courage to do that. So forming alliances in the networking scene is a very useful strategy, as your alliances look out for you, introduce you and refer you to others (and vice versa). They are also very handy people to approach and say hello to when you first get to an event and you find that don't know very many people!

Forming alliances is done over time. Alliances share the same values, way of doing business or are like minded to you. You must build trust with them and deliver results. Once you have done this consistently, your alliances will back you, endorse you and suggest you for projects and opportunities.

6. Creative thinking

When someone shares information with you it may open a door inside your head to a fantastic idea. If you can, have a small notebook in your bag or briefcase to capture ideas.

Also try and remain creative when speaking and listening to others. They may not see an opportunity or an idea and you can point them out.

Doors open in many different ways when you are thinking creatively and people want to be around others who can create ideas, create results and be able to relate on many levels.

I was at a community event recently where I was actively listening to the people talking about a particular issue. I suggested an idea that they considered and ultimately used in their solution. I don't get any benefit from that idea directly, however, the people in that group have asked me to contribute to other ideas and community programs. This invitation to contribute has opened doors to networks and groups of leaders in other fields I normally don't have access to, which will be very valuable indeed!

7. Momentum – start slow at first

Many people go to a few events and get disillusioned with their 'results'. I have often heard people complain that their networking is not paying off and they are "wasting time and money to go to all of these events".

My advice is: keep the big picture in mind – your overall intention. Networking is like a snowball. You get small results at first (referrals, introductions, leads) and when it's rolling down the hill, then the results get bigger and better as it gets moving (new clients, opportunities, deals, strategic introductions).

Remember, if the 'results' came in thick and fast at the start of joining a network, would you be ready for them? Most people wouldn't be, as you need to have systems in place to follow up and deliver. Plus, relationship building takes time for people to know and trust each other. The investment of time for a new network to give you results (depending on you and the network you are joining) can be from 3 to 12 months.

Always remember the three P's:
patience, persistence and participation.

If you're not getting the results you want, you might want to check the effectiveness of your networking style, etiquette, your intentions, attitude, language, phone messages, general behaviour and lastly your own generosity to the network you want to be a part of.

If you don't come up with any answers as to why your networking isn't working, go and ask for suggestion from someone in the network that you have met. They may give you honest feedback that you may not want to hear. If you are committed to being part of the network, take on the feedback and make some changes. Remember to thank the person who told you the truth. They didn't have to and you'll be glad they did.

Chapter 6

THE BIG QUESTIONS ANSWERED

How do you work a room?

How do you keep moving?

How do you remember names?

The person you came to meet

How do you juggle food/drinks and cards?

How do I get out of a corner?

Why do I have to network?

When can I stop networking?

How do you work a room?

When I ask people in my workshops and seminars this question, the answers are as follows:

Walk around and meet people; don't get pushed into a corner; make yourself known by talking really loud; get lots of business cards; talk to everyone before they all go; do lots of business; don't let people leave until you get the sale!

When it comes to working a room, my advice is....DON'T work it. Do not even try to meet everybody. The networking philosophy I stick to is:

The most important person in the room that you can speak to is... right in front of you.

7 steps to working a room

The best way I have found to work a room is:

1   Before entering the room, stop, breathe and let go of trying to 'make it happen'

2   Walk into the room. Yes, you must go in!

3   When inside, go up to someone and say,

    'Hello, my name is…, what's yours?'

4   Ask them why they came to the event/function and be interested in their response

5   Ask them another question about them. The less talking about you the better. That doesn't mean you don't say anything – quite the contrary. You want to ensure that what you say has impact and is not boring

6   Be relaxed and open to the discovery of new people. You never know who you're going to meet next!

7   Say hello to another person and start again.

How do you keep moving?

Keep focussed on why you are there. If your intention is to meet a certain number of people, to introduce five other people to each other, or even make sure the event is running to schedule... keep remembering that.

If you feel you are stuck in a conversation that is not progressing you any further, excuse yourself from the group when there is a pause. A great way to do that is to say, "I have enjoyed this conversation, thank you, I'm going to keep moving." Sometimes, you don't have to say anything at all. When there is a pause, just gently move out of the circle, go and get some refreshments and join another group or start talking to another person.

Remember, people won't be offended if you move around. Networking is like being in a butterfly house. Some butterflies will land on your shoulder, others will be collecting nectar from flowers away from you and others are just sitting in the sun. You can't force a butterfly to land on you. Be yourself at these events and if you feel you need to move, don't make a drama about it, just move.

If you find yourself standing alone, don't start talking to yourself, go meet someone. A good way to do this is find someone and introduce yourselves. You have no idea who the person really is until you start talking to them. You have no idea who they know or what possibilities they can open to you or - more importantly what you can offer them now and in the future.

What about flirting & attraction?

Occasionally you may find you are attracted to someone and/or they are flirting with you! How do you handle this?

If you are interested in pursuing conversation with this person at a later date, remember the reason you have come to the event. – YOUR intention! Don't squander all your time on this one person. Just make sure you have exchanged cards, have gleaned a little information about them and they about you, and that you have let them know you would like to contact them again. Maybe even after the event has finished. REMEMBER – don't be too eager!! Keep some mystery that will make that person want to be in touch with you again – soon!

And what if you do not appreciate their flirting? Spend a short time with them, thank them for their time and move on. It is as easy as that. Remember why you came to the event!

Note:

If you have experienced flirting at an event and for any reason feel ucomfortable to leave on your own, have a trusted friend to walk you to your car or the train or call a taxi to pick you up right out front.

Networking is about being safe and it's always best to be cautious and trust your instincts.

How do you remember names?

There are various ways to improve your memory of people's names such as:

• Say their name when you are introduced to them.

• Repeat their first name when you're talking to them – just don't overdo it and don't make it sound weird! Just drop the name into the conversation as naturally as you can. This takes practice, and it reinforces the name for you and strengthens your connection with the other person.

• Write their name on a card with something memorable they have said or something you want to remember about them.

• Use self-talk. Tell yourself over and over every day that your memory is great, you remember names the first time you hear them – and you will! You can even programme your mind before a networking event by saying this to yourself again and again in the car on the way there.

- Remember the person, not the name. There are going to be times when you see someone you know you've had a conversation with before, and you can't remember their name, no matter how hard you try. Say to them, "You know, your face is so familiar, and I just can't remember your name". When you say that to someone, they'll forgive you right there and then, because they know that you do remember them and you're simply having a mental block, which is much better than trying to cover it up.

How do you talk to the person you came to meet?

We often go to events to hear a particular speaker or meet with someone who is a VIP or centre of influence person.

When you want to talk to them, they may be talking to someone else. When that happens, stand back a bit from them so they can see you, and just wait.

They know that people will want to talk to them and they will on occasion look around. When they do, catch their eye and smile and they will acknowledge you are there and talk to you next.

If you don't catch their eye after waiting for about five minutes or so, they may be in the middle of a conversation they don't want to break. If that happens, you have to choose what you do. Ask yourself how important it is for you to meet this person right now. If it's very important, your options are:

- Keep waiting to catch their eye
- Go and do something else and come back
- Interrupt their conversation.

I'll leave it up to your discretion how appropriate the last option is. On the whole it is rude, and I don't suggest it, however there are always special circumstances.

My advice here is to think about your intention and understand the impact your interruption will have on the people you are interrupting before you act.

How do you juggle your glass and food & business card?

Now this is a hard one! Try to keep one hand free to shake hands. You can do this by holding your glass and any food in one hand and keep your cards in your right pocket. The secret here is to always wear something with an accessible right pocket and also not to be eating or drinking too much food so you have free hands.

If you want to write on a card, either put the glass etc on a table or ask the other person to hold your glass for you while you write. You may have the opportunity to then repay the courtesy and hold their glass while they write details about you. It all adds to remembering a particular person apart from others.

How do you handle extra bags?

You don't want to worry about your bags, nor do you want to lug them around all night. Put as much down as possible in a secure place. Have a bag with a shoulder strap to leave your hands free.

How do I get out of the corner in the room?

Politely excuse yourself from whoever you are talking to and move on. For those of you who end up in the corner feeling overwhelmed by everything, take a deep breath and start moving towards a specific point in the room – that could be the food, the drinks or a display. You want to get out of the corner as you will be hard to find and the 'flow' of people moving around is not as much on the edge, as it is towards the centre of the room. If you stand in a corner or on the edge, you are watching networking, not being in it. You came to network – take the plunge and go and say hello to someone.

Why do I have to network?

Networking is all about meeting people and having conversations. We do it all the time and don't even know it. For example, did you say hello to someone on the way to work, when picking up your child from school, buying lunch or going to the supermarket? I bet you did.

If you had only exchanged saying hello, that is a basic form of networking. If you happen to meet that person again in the same situation, you might share more about each other and build a relationship – that is what networking is all about. It's not an onerous task, it's something you do naturally anyway, so the concept of 'having to network' is irrelevant as we do it all the time.

> Just because you have a career change doesn't mean networking is over - it means the game has changed and there are new people to meet and support. Enjoy!

When can I stop networking?

Networking and communicating with other people are a way of life. You can only stop networking if you become a hermit, disconnect the phone, internet, and mobile phone, go to a silent meditation retreat or DIE! Get the point?

There will be times in your life when the level of networking is slow and other times it seems fast. There are many situations that can affect the type of networking you do, such as retirement, leaving work to have a baby, taking extended leave to care for a relative or friend, or even going on holiday.

You won't necessarily 'network' for work purposes, and you will meet people in your new area of focus who will be able to assist you. The fun part about career shifts and life changes is that you never know until it happens, how the people you meet in one area of your life can make a massive contribution to another.

My grandmother Polly has been retired for quite a few years now. That has not stopped her being an active networker. Polly is a member of OWN - the Older Women's Network and she's taught herself desktop design, Mandarin Chinese and Spanish. She walks most Wednesdays with 'Wednesday Walkers' and participates in many social and cultural events in Sydney where she lives.

Can this woman network - you bet. She's so much of a fan of my work that she takes my business cards with her. I got an email a few months ago from a successful business owner in Sydney that wanted to meet me after hearing Polly talk about what I do in her shop! Totally awesome. Who do you know that's changed career's that you could support and network with?

Chapter 7

WHAT DOES NOT WORK!

Gossiping with others

Talking about yourself all the time

Taking everyone's cards in a frenzy

Watching the room

Waiting for perfect!

There are some simple do's and don'ts when networking. Let's begin with what doesn't work.

Gossiping with others

Refrain from gossip or saying anything bad about anyone, EVER!

There are many reasons for this:

- You end up looking bad

- The credibility and reputation of the person you are gossiping about is damaged by the gossip

- The person you are gossiping with will not trust that you won't do the same to them.

If you find yourself in a conversation that is gossip, change the conversation or walk away from the group and encourage others to do the same. You do not have time to belittle others!

Talking about yourself all the time

It is OK to talk about yourself some of the time. People who go on about themselves are painful and boring. Just make sure you are listening twice as much as speaking. Remember, you have two ears and one mouth, use them in that proportion!

Taking everyone's cards in a frenzy

Networking is about building relationships. When you meet someone and get their card, THAT is the moment to start the relationship. If you collect 50 cards in an hour, you won't remember who you met, they won't remember you, and it's harder to build a relationship.

Watching the room for 'more important people'

This is frustrating for the person you are talking to. Please, respect them. If you are talking to them, be with them. If you are actually waiting for someone else and can't concentrate on another person, let that person know what is happening and ask if they mind you keeping an eye out in this way while you talk.

If you are the host of an event or have a specific role at the event, let the person you are speaking with know. Such as... "Cath, I'm the organiser of today's event and I need to be available to greet the Keynote Speaker. I'm happy to speak quickly with you now, however if we get interrupted, I'm happy to talk after this event. Is that OK with you?"

Waiting for perfect!

This is my pet favorite Don't DO! It is when you are not in action because everything isn't quite right or... perfect! I know about this because I do it and so do many people I speak with. Remember,

- You are who you are!
- You look like YOU (tall, short, fat, pretty, bald, young...)
- You have the business card you've got
- You know what you know
- You've had the day that you've had.

Accept yourself and your situation and go out there and meet people. If you wait for perfect, you will do nothing and regret it later.

Perfection will make you happy and at the same time will get you nowhere really fast !

WHAT DOES WORK

Having an intention

Being excited

Sharing yourself and being real

Handing out your cards

Asking and giving referrals

What's The Best Thing?™

Be generous with your listening

Give referrals

Follow up

Building community

WOW SHE REALLY KNOWS WHAT SHE IS TALKING ABOUT

Having an intention

As I explained earlier, if you know what you want from the event or meeting, you will have a better experience. Intentions are great. Examples could be:

- I am going to meet five new people at the event

- I am going to introduce five people to each other

- I am going to have fun

- I am going to learn something new

- I am not going to eat the dessert at the dinner!

Being excited

Excitement is catchy. If you are excited and positive, others who are excited and positive will be attracted to you. Being excited means that you are open and receptive. You will hear others better and that means you will be in a frame of mind to create more opportunities. Being excited also enables you to deal with people who are not interested in anything – you pick up their spirits because you are so positive. Be wary of this type of person – they can drain your energy! Give them your time and move on if they are not contributing to the 'conversation'. Just the fact of your being there might ignite a spark in them that makes it all worthwhile.

Sharing yourself and being real

When you are genuine with another person rather than 'full of it', they can tell you are being real. The quality of the relationship you build with them will be enhanced if you are sharing yourself. When I say share yourself, I don't mean bare your soul and tell them your whole life history! Sharing yourself is when you bring in a little piece of your life to the conversation. (Remember the List of Confidences you did earlier.)

Handing out your cards

If someone asks you for your card – give it to them. Don't make them beg for it or tease them that they might get it at the end of the evening (yes, sadly, I've seen people do that).

Also, if you are in a conversation that has been going for 10 minutes or more and you are interested in talking to them more, ask for their business card and organise to follow up with them after the event.

Asking and giving referrals

Giving referrals works. Networking is all about relationships and you may be able to help the person you have just met. Make connections and introduce people to each other. They will remember your assistance. Also, when someone has referred a contact or opportunity to you, respond straight away and thank them by phone, fax, a nice card or email. Your intention is to acknowledge the referrer and keep them up to date with how everything is going.

What's the Best Thing?™

I have found a bullet proof way of interrupting someone else's day drama. It works for me every time and I'd like to share it with you. Its called…What's The Best Thing?™ It is not about being a Pollyanna, a master of positive thinking or a psychologist. The intention is to get someone out of their day drama for just a moment to appreciate life and get into the present. It won't change them permanently, however what it does do, is shift their focus and their mental state so that you can interact with them on a more positive and productive level.

What's the Best Thing exercise!

OK – the person you are talking to is going on and on about their day and they are getting more negative by the second (Day drama in overdrive!). You want to create conversation, not get sucked into complaining about life in general. Your purpose for going to a networking event is to meet people and create opportunity for yourself and others. So here is what to do...

1. Think about the best thing that has happened to you today. Once you have thought about it, really appreciate it and smile to yourself

2. When the other person has taken a breath before launching into another drama ask them...

   "Can I ask you a question?"

   The will usually reply with "Yes"

   Ask them, "What is the best thing that has happened to you today?" and then gently smile at them and wait for an answer

3. Most of the time what happens is, they look at you blankly and say "What?" If they do that, gently and sincerely repeat the question

4. Then, the person will scan their memory looking for the best thing. You'll know they've found something because they smile and look at you and tell you what it is.

Some people may find this exercise confronting to do. That's fine. However, I've done this hundreds of times and I assure you nobody has ever yelled at me to mind my own business when I've done this. Some people have really had to think to find something good, and there's always something.

Some of the responses I have received are:

"What's good was, I woke up"

"I watched my daughter take her first steps"

"I got flowers today"

"I had a fantastic lunch – my partner made it for me"

"Jennifer, thanks – I forgot how great my life is and I didn't come tonight to burden everyone with the moans of my life!"

"I made a sale. Now what about YOU, Miss Positive, what's the best thing that's happened to you today?"

People will ask you about your best thing, so be ready. Your response and theirs to the question is enough to start a conversation. Remember, whatever a person's answer to the question is, accept it. It is THEIR best thing and they have just lifted their focus to what's good in the world – so do not judge their response, just go with the flow.

BONUS NOTE:

I have had people come back to me and tell me they have done this exercise at home with the family, including the children at dinner. Everyone comes to dinner with a Best Thing and that is the conversation starter. Everyone gets to participate and everyone learns more about each other. It's a great way to build your family relationships, encourage conversation that's not about TV, school or work gossip and celebrate achievements.

You can also do this exercise at work as a starter for a team meeting or a planning day. For example, what's the best about our team, our department, our company, your role in the company? Give it a try and see what kind of results you get.

If you've get some interesting responses and want to share them, I've set up a website called www.whatsthebestthing.com. Log on and post your experiences. I'd love to read them and share them with others!

Be generous with your listening

Most of the time, people focus on what they are dealing with and how they are dealing with it. They don't focus outside of themselves. This is not good or bad, it's just the way things are. When you are generously listening to others, you listen to where they are coming from – not what they are saying.

In other words, try to listen to what's behind their words and comments. What is on the outside may not reflect what's going on inside another person's head.

When people say things, remember to not take anything personally – it's rarely going to be about you!

I was at a business networking function. A very well-dressed man in a suit was looking a little uncomfortable. I thought that was a little unusual as he looked like he was a CEO and had been to events like this many times before.

I approached him and introduced myself. His name was Bill. I asked Bill why he had come to the event. His response was, 'Well, I came to this network to meet interesting, dynamic people.' I could have left it there, however behind the words and watching his body language, there was more. As I asked Bill a few more question. It turned out that Bill had been a stay at home dad for the last five years and before he became a full time parent, he had been a well-regarded business leader.

Bill hadn't been in the business world nor to a networking function for what seemed to him a very long time and he was very nervous. This was not clear when I asked him why he came to the event.

Listening behind the words can support other people and help them network and build their confidence.

We didn't do any business on the night, however Bill is a good contact for me and he's thrilled I was there to support his return to the world of business.

Give referrals

You are at a networking event to learn, share and experience. Pay attention to the people you are meeting. Not all of them will be able to assist you or you assist them right now.

However, people you meet at the event may be able to assist each other. You have a fantastic opportunity to be an advocate for someone else in the room. Listen to what people want and help them get what they want!

Be on the lookout for needs and see how you can fill them through the people you meet and resources you have access to.

I was at my very first networking event in Bendigo, Victoria. Before the evening started I began talking to a man who had come from Melbourne. His name was Don Cook and he's an executive recruitment specialist. I told him that I work with businesses to increase their sales, help them grow and that I write business plans for growing companies. We exchanged business cards and then I didn't see Don for the rest of the night.

During this same event, Warrick Smith from Grabstick approached me. He had my card. He said, 'Jennifer, I met Don Cook a few minutes ago and told him about my business . Don gave me your card and suggested I speak to you.'

Now, Don couldn't help Warrick directly in their initial meeting and could see that I might be able to. As a result of that introduction, I have worked with Warrick and also developed a strategic alliance with Don and his business. Don's generous referral created benefit for Warrick and countless others at that event, and even now in this book!

Follow up

How many people have said they would call you and never did? How many times have you wanted something someone else had, you were prepared to spend your time and money with them, and they never followed up with you?

The number one key to networking is to keep your promises and follow up! Do what you say you are going to do. Be realistic with your promises. If you know it will take you a week to do something, say so – don't be too eager and promise you can deliver in 24 hours when you know that's not possible. Under promise and over deliver!

Also, remember your current commitments before making new ones. When you are true to yourself and your commitments, others respect you and opportunity flows to you.

If you have trouble remembering what you said you will do, here are some ideas to help you remember:

- Write the action on the back of the person's business card when you are with them, talking to them. Don't do it at the end of the meeting or event, as you are likely to forget.

- Have a little notepad in your pocket or purse and write the action down.

- Use your diary or electronic PDA and put the action on your to-do list.

Whatever your strategy, you may feel a little silly doing this when you're still with the person you are talking to. However, they will appreciate your follow-up and that you keep your commitments. This will build their confidence in YOU which means they will be more likely to do business with you and refer you to others.

Chapter 9

BUILDING COMMUNITY

See and commit to a bigger picture

Add value, not ego!

Build links and connections

Be a community advocate

Invest in community ventures

Create and grow leaders

Achievement and success

If one of your intentions in networking is to build the local community you live and/or work in, you will be successful and so will your community.

Advanced networking, or what I like to call proactive networking skills, Is for the truly passionate who are deeply committed to long term success for themselves and their community.

The 7 Keys to Proactive Networking are;

1.   See & commit to a bigger picture

2.   Add value, not ego!

3.   Build links and connections into many points of the community

4.   Be a community advocate

5.   Invest in community ventures

6.   Create and grow leaders

7.   Acknowledge the success and achievements of others.

See and commit to a bigger picture

We tend to see the world from our perspective most of the time, especially when there are hard times, cash flow crisis, family and /or health issues challenging us or the people we love.

Proactive networkers usually have found a vision that inspires them, that they want to see become real in their community / in business and/or in their life. They become what I call a 'champion' for seeing a change, development or result in their community, business or place of work and life. They stay locked into that vision and all the little distractions and problems of day to day life are systematically dealt with so they can move towards realising their bigger vision/ goal.

For example, my vision is seeing families and businesses working together to create peace and profit. I see many business owners and business leaders working on their own (yes, not proactively networking), doing long hours, all in the name of providing for the family and most often than not, the result is they loose their family through divorce or separation. Where's the peace and joy in that??? There is none.

Peace and Profit is the vision I have, whereby families stay together and the parent or parents generate enough income so they have balance, decent profit and a joyful, peaceful family life. (I realise there will be normal non-joyful and non-peaceful family moments, what I am envisioning however is the overall experience that families have is peace and profit, not despair, depression and family breakdown).

So, what is your vision / commitment to your community on a local, national and international level that inspires you? If you don't know, just start with your local community and create a vision for that.

What is your vision?

_____

_____

_____

_____

_____

_____

_____

_____

_____

_____

Add value, not ego!

When proactive networkers have conversations they add value and see the benefit in teamwork. Networking is not about big noting yourself or even, at times, wanting recognition for your contribution. Now that said, recognition is important, however experienced networkers know that part of the responsibility of moving closer to their vision and the end result, is more important than acknowledgement and recognition.

What are you prepared to let go of to achieve your vision?

_____

_____

_____

_____

_____

_____

_____

_____

_____

Build links and connections into many parts of the community

Real success in a community comes when everyone is engaged. As a leader, you want as many people connected and inspired about your vision. Share your vision simply and often, with anyone that will listen in. The reason for doing this is to create momentum and have as many people as possible who are inspired by the vision and who can contribute to it. Never underestimate any person, position, age, demographic or the potential of another person. Your prime objective is to share the vision, engage as many people as possible to participate and get results. Proactive Networkers do not have time for discrimination, exclusion or gossip. They focus on results and spreading the vision and word of what they stand for.

Be a community advocate

You want to promote the community you are in everywhere you go. Now, as you may have noticed, I have promoted Bendigo, Victoria, Australia quite a bit in this book. There is a reason for doing this and the reason is: I am passionate about Bendigo and will promote it everywhere I go. I get benefit from it and the Bendigo 'brand' and community benefit from me doing that too.

As you can probably tell, I am also an advocate for my family, other businesses and family success in the world. When you are being a community advocate, you generate interest, awareness and create opportunities for your community group outside of your home community. When you are an advocate you become a magnet attracting ideas, people, innovation, resources and opportunity into your community. Who benefits from this? Your community AND YOU!

Invest in community ventures

As a business owner or wage earner, I encourage you to invest in your community and networks. You can do this financially by sponsoring events, certain individuals or projects. You can also do this by donating some of your time, resources or equipment to the community / network activity.

I take great delight doing this as I can see direct benefits to me and my company as well as investing in the community as a whole.

An example of a commuity venture

His Holiness the Dali Lama is coming to Bendigo in June this year to bless the largest Stupa that has been built in the southern hemisphere. Only a few businesses were asked to financially sponsor and contribute to the visit. Now this visit is a very big deal for Bendigo and Australia. It's also a big deal for me. How many times will I be able to experience such an event and also attend a small reception with the Dali Lama in Australia?

Answer - not many, if ever.

So my company has made a sponsorship contribution to the visit. The benefit in doing this keeps the cost down for the several thousand people that will come to Bendigo and pay for a ticket to hear him speak. This is an event for the entire community and if they benefit, so do I.

Also, my close friend Gerri's goal this year is to experience several 'once in a lifetime' dreams. As I get two tickets with my sponsoship, Gerri has accepted my invitation to attend. I'm delighted that I can make one of her dreams come true.

I love how this works, I urge you to get involved in your community.

Create and grow leaders

Leaders are everywhere - from people who are actively out in front with the vision and mission blazing, to the more simple, yet another type of effective leader who takes initiative to diffuse an argument between to people, solve a long standing problem or develop an innovative idea.

Leadership comes in many ways and proactive networkers are continually on the lookout to foster, encourage and develop emerging leaders in the community. The reality is that networks and community groups need succession, and the long term success of your vision will depend on how well you have involved your community in the vision and enabled them to contribute to it.

Proactive networkers are able to convert the vision and share it with many people to pursue the vision. They take great joy and delight in watching other leaders realise the vision or achieve the result. Everyone then owns the result and is empowered by it.

For those of you that don't know, Bendigo now has its own bank! The Bendigo Bank (at the time of printing) has a market capitalisation of approximately $1.9 billion (340 branches, more than 3300 staff, and $16 billion in assets under management). The man currently leading the bank is Mr Rob Hunt AM. Rob is the Managing Director of the Bendigo Bank Group and is a visionary and innovative leader who embodies this type of advanced networking skill and thinking.

Rob started working in the Bendigo Building Society in 1973. He's been in the company for over 30 years and knows what it takes to build a vision, a successful business and create and lead a community. I had the opportunity to interview Rob last year at a Young Entrepreneur's Forum and his insight on leadership and building community for anyone in business was:

- be passionate about what you do and go in to make a difference

- keep the vision firmly in your mind in a way that inspires you

- identify, nurture and encourage emerging leaders in your team and community

- understand you're ability to lead versus manage

- share the vision piece by piece and create the steps to realise the big picture

- be patient and realistic in building the vision.

Acknowledge others' achievement and success

This point really is straight forward. If someone in your network is successful, congratulate them and recognise their achievements. Too often, people will not do this as they feel inadequate or jealous at someone else's great results. This is not productive for you or your network community. You can acknowledge others in many ways effectively;

- Newspaper announcement
- Send them a hand written note
- Send them an email
- Announce their achievement at an event or gathering
- Take them to lunch or dinner
- Give them a token or gift.

Acknowledgement is all about recognising greatness in another and that they have achieved something special and important (to them and the network/community as a whole).

Remember the key to successful community networking is ...

I want what you want!

Whatever someone else wants, want it for them and wherever you can, help them get it either directly or indirectly. I have used this concept many times and without fail, it has worked.

I have many examples where I have wanted for others 'what they wanted' and gone about making that happen. For example, more sales for their business, time out of the business for a holiday, a better book-keeper or accountant, an introduction to a VIP In business, to quit their corporate job and start a business.

So whatever my clients, family, friends, community or network want, I will do my best every time to see if I can help make that happen. I don't look for recognition, getting something in return or believing my generosity will repay me ten-fold.

Why do I do this? It's because it's the right thing to do and everyone benefits from the results, every time.

Always remember,
networking replaces the work hard factor.

It's all about practice, patience and persistence!

Now that you have read this book and gained some insight as to how you could network more effectively, creating communities and networks around you, I encourage you to take action and make it happen.

NETWORKING TOOLS

Business Cards
For business cards that are VERY affordable, excellent quality and fast delivery...
www.businesscards.net.au

Handbags / Wallets / Purses
For stunning bags, luggage and accessories, I suggest Catherine Manuell Designs
http://www.catherinemanuelldesign.com

Example networks to consider

Most of these networks will exist in your local community. I have gone to most
of the examples of the networks listed below at some point in my life and
participated in events to 'try on' the network to see if it was a fit for me.
I encourage you to go these networks in your local community visit them
and see if they work for you.

Service Clubs

> Rotary Australia
> Lions Australia
> YsMen International
> Apex

Womens Networks

> Australian Businesswomen's Network
> Rural Women's Network
> The Older Women's Network
> Zonta International
> Informal Women's Networks

Business Groups

> Business Network International
> SWAP (Sales People With a Purpose)
> Chamber of Commerce
> Micro Business Network
> Institute of Chartered Accountants
> Franchise Council of Australia
>
> Business Enterprise Centres
> Australian Institute of Office Professionals

Business Groups

Australian Human Resources Institute
Australian Institute of Company Directors (AICD)
Australian Institute of Management

Sporting Groups

Football Club, Soccer Club
Netball Association
Tennis, Cricket, Swimming
Lawn Bowls

Special Interest Networks

Computer / Internet Club
Playgroup - Mums & Babies
Pottery & Craft
Languages

Charities

Hospital Auxiliaries
Make a Wish Foundation
Cancer Support Groups
Salvation Army

Religious Networks

Anglican / Catholic / Baptist / Hindu / Muslim
Baha'i Faith

Recreational Networks

Local Gym
Car clubs / 4WD adventures
Scrap booking networks
Singing / photography

Education

Adult Education Courses & Programs
University / TAFE Courses & Programs
Post Grad Courses – eg MBAs
Business Seminars & Courses
Motivational Seminars

Personal Development Programs

Landmark Education - www.landmarkeduaction.com
Success and You - www.successandyou.com.au

FURTHER ACKNOWLEDGEMENTS

Robyn Henderson - Global Networking Specialist and Publisher.
I was inspired by Robyn over 15 years ago when I went to my first networking event as an employee in Sydney. I was 22, had made my own business cards and I was the only person in the room that had a card. Robyn's words of encouragement way back then and over the years to keep growing, developing and shining as brightly as I could have never left me. Robyn you are an angel, thank you.

The Bendigo Community
I've lived in many places and there is something very special about Bendigo. The sense of community, the collaborative spirit, the innovation, commercial savvy and creativity is just incredible. The community has a very humble nature and just gets on with the job, not looking for really looking for recognition or acknowledgement. I think that is why Bendigo creates national and world champions in all areas of life. To the Bendigo Community, I am truly grateful for being welcomed so generously and encouraged to contribute to the present and future success for us all.

Donna Collier, Regional Development Victoria
Donna is a consummate networker who creates opportunity for others wherever she goes. Donna, thank you for your belief in me and taking a punt to see if I could deliver results when I first moved to Bendigo. Success breeds success and it has been great fun creating the results for local businesses and young entrepreneurs in the projects we have worked on together. You are an extraordinary business woman!

Lilly Miszewski and Brian Gould - City of Greater Bendigo
Thank you both for backing me and endorsing me when I first moved to Bendigo. It takes courage to back a stranger in a new town and I am delighted to have delivered, with you, successful Business Planning Programs and other local business development activities in the region to grow local businesses and the community.

Leah MacLean, Coach/Mentor and extraordinary business woman
Leah, you were a true champion by keeping my dream to publish this book alive. If you had not got me into action, this book would not be in your hands now! Thank you.

The Central Victorian Business Network - www.cvbn.org.au
An exceptional organisation that I am so proud to be a part of. This organisation
has networking down to an art, and they do it naturally. To the Chairman, Craig
Hunter, and my fellow members of the Committee of Management, I am so
impressed with how you operate and how you want to create opportunities
for others and the region at large. You are an inspiring team and I'm certain
the members of the network appreciate all your efforts to ensure that Bendigo
businesses and the community at large, grow and are successful.

Wendi Nutt, Owner, Philadelphia Philpot - www.philadelphiaphilpot.com
Wendy is the Hat lady at the event I went to in Mosman, Sydney. Her fabulous
couture hats & headpieces for race days, brides, mothers of the bride, theatrical
events & TV commercials are stunning. Wendi's motto is "Radiate presence - wear
a hat!" Wendy, thank you for your inspiration and courage to be authentic when
promoting your product. You have inspired many in my seminars and now, through
this book, I can repay the gesture by promoting you!

Glennis Brooking, South East Community College - www.secc.nsw.edu.au
Glennis, the NSW South Coast networking master. Glennis, the Art of Networking
came to life with the Women in Business Mentor Program. I could see how much
of a difference it could make to people everywhere. This book is due to your
wanting to make a difference to other women in business and your enthusiasm
and passion for excellence. Thank you for your ongoing support and creating a Jen
Harwood fan club on the South Coast!

Peter Reading, Sign-A-Rama Bendigo - www.signarama.com.au
Peter is one of those people who are community advocates. Yes, he most definitely
wants to grow his business and he does that through building and fostering his
community. Peter, thank you for inviting me to my first local Bendigo event and
supporting me as I grew the Bendigo arm of the business.

Don Cook, Haymes Cook & Associates - www.haymescook.com
Don is an advanced networker. Actively listening and seeing where he can add
value to others. He takes great pride and joy seeing others grow and develop. His
business is based in Melbourne specialising in executive recruitment. Don, you
are a legend and it a pleasure knowing you.

Never forget where you came from and always
acknowledge those who helped realise your dreams!

ABOUT THE AUTHOR

Jennifer Harwood is the 2006 Inaugural Kerrie Nairn National Scholarship Winner for public speaking developed by the National Speakers Association of Australia and the Federal Department of Education and Training. Jennifer's other national career award was as a young entrepreneur in 1998 where Jennifer and her team won the National Winner for Best Business Plan, Best Financial Plan through the Enterprise Development Institute of Australia and AusIndustry. Jennifer is committed to excellence in all that she undertakes.

Jennifer's company, Jen Harwood Pty Ltd is a national business development firm specialising in growing businesses and their owners to increase their sales, profits and leadership effectiveness. Jennifer founded her company at 29 years of age and has built an impressive team and client base over the last 11 years. The company's innovative business coaching, consulting, training and business development products are practical, informative and motivational for business owners and their teams. With Jen Harwood Pty Ltd as your 'silent' business partner, you ensure success.

Jennifer puts back into the business community regularly. She is a recognised mentor to growing businesses through many Women in Business Mentor Programmes, the Young Achievers Australia Programme, and regional business community groups. Her company sponsors local events, business and community projects. Jennifer is committed to active participation in business and community development.

This woman walks her talk!

email jen@jenharwood.com or visit the website at www.jenharwood.com

Motivational Speaker

Jennifer Harwood is an avalanche of inspiring energy and enthusiasm!

Your audiences will be moved, touched and inspired to grow their businesses, think beyond mediocrity and get the best out of life.

Jennifer's background enables her to present tailored keynote addresses and seminars to suit the audience and client requirements. Her extensive knowledge of people and business ensures that her presenting style is engaging, fun, informative and results oriented. Your participants will walk away with inspiration, motivation and most importantly strategies to get results from the moment they leave the event.

Jennifer's workshops add value and build on Conference themes so your participants can explore deeper into the subject focus, turn ideas into strategies and take action immediately.

Below are proven workshops and seminars that Jennifer has developed to get results.

How to Attract the Ideal Client

What to look for in a client & how to approach

How to secure long term business

What to say in the moment of opportunity

How to say NO to the wrong deal

Super Sales & Smiling Customers

How to sell through the price block

Service isn't enough – How to create experiences

How to understand your customer better

How to increase profits with minimal change

Getting Family & Business to Work!

How to balance business and family
Building the team outside family
Family rules for business and vice versa
Managing business roles and accountability

The Art of Networking

How to build your business & potential customers
How to find and attract the ideal customer
How to target what you want
How to ask AND get what you want

Home Based Business is about Attitude!

Create the right impression first time, every time
Know the 10 keys to a successful home business.
How to work with BIG business from a HOME base
How to Network and Partner for success from home.

5 Business Planning Keys to Get Results!

How to set a compelling vision, goals and actions
Getting the plan and strategy clear with the team
How to get results, not just talk about them
What it takes to grow and keep great people

How to Survive and Thrive in Tough Times

In tough times business owners need clarity and focus. There is little room for daydreaming, procrastination and expensive punts to try something new.

The 5 areas for keeping control and focus in your business are:
* Get Real – know where you are, where your going and what you need
* Listen to the Market – it's not about you, what do your customer want
* Re-design, Re-package or Re-invent
* Engage – learn how to connect, market and sell
* Review – test results; collect feedback and learn how to get over yourself when you get stuck!

Jen has worked with hundreds of business owners to get through tough times and ensure that they are stronger, more balanced and ready to handle any challenge.

Small Business on a Budget

Many small businesses fail because they are great at earning money and poor at managing it. The 5 areas for small business financial success are:

* Spending – knowing what to buy, when to buy it, and for how much
* Pricing – learn how to price your products and services for maximum profit
* Saving – learn how to create cushions of support even when cash-flow is slow
* Debt – learn how to have debt and still sleep soundly at night
* Advice – knowing what to ask and who to ask for quality information

Being organised and money savvy is essential for success. Jen's experience on managing money, credit card debt and cash-flow in her own business and with clients will inspire you to get your finances under control.

Training – Custom Designed Business Workshops & Programs

Jennifer's experience gives her the ability to custom design informative, interactive and dynamic workshops and seminars to meet clients KPIs and specific results.

Examples include::

Sales Essentials for Retailers – Sales basics for retail sales staff

The Selling & Buying Process – Understand how buying & selling to get results

Start-up RIGHT so you don't stop! – How to build your business from scratch

The Entrepreneurs Game – Team building and entrepreneurial training workshop

The Confident Woman – How to be confident at work and get the results you want

Business Development Manager Success – Maximising your results

Public Speaking Basics Workshop – How to speak in public without feeling silly

What Customers Want – How to give TOP customer service

Making A Difference – How one person can make a difference !

First Impressions of your Business – Marketing Strategies for every business

"Jennifer achieved outstanding results through her keynote address focussing on the 'What and How', and workshops two days later at the conference focussing on 'How to do it'. Our retailers, through surveys, have told us this conference was the best they have attended and that Jennifer provided not just the inspiration, but also the confidence and tools to implement many things that have improved the efficiency and profitability of their businesses, as well as putting back the fun. On the whole, they now work more proactively in partnership with BioLab Australia. Jennifer more than met our expectations and moreover was a delight to work with through the entire project."

Rob Wilson, Marketing & Retail Manager – Aust/NZ, BioLab Australia.

"We asked Jennifer to stimulate the participants' thinking about what we do well, but also about how we might change and become sustainable and grow. Jennifer obviously did considerable research about our organisation before the event. Jennifer contacted the international leadership and posed questions that have stimulated them to think about issues more than they had done before. Jennifer impressed the participants with her knowledge of our organisation, and initiated the change in thinking that we had sought. This was done in such a way that very few raised concerns about changes being made by the leaders during the remainder of the convention. Jennifer's address finished with a standing ovation, something many participants have not seen before. The address was the highlight of the weekend for many participants."

Colin Lambie, Australian Regional Director, International Association of Y'sMens Club Inc

"Thank you for being the Master of Ceremonies for our recent conference entitled Stepping Forward, Stepping Up. It was clear to me that you had put a lot of thought and preparation into your role and this together with your warmth, energy and boundless enthusiasm made for a highly motivating and interactive day of learning. You are a true professional committed to achieving successful outcomes for stakeholders".

Christina Cummins, Director, Inspiring Events.

JEN HARWOOD PTY LTD

Jen Harwood Pty Ltd offers 3 areas of business development services. They are:

- Business Coaching
- Business Consulting
- Business Planning Programs

Business Coaching

When you're at the top blazing a new future for yourself, your family, your customers or the world, it's easy to miss the little stuff essential in planning, implementation and maintaining balance of all areas of your life. The key to success is thinking, communication and action. Our business coaching services are essential to serious and committed people growing their business and careers. Each coach/mentor is matched specifically to you so that their experience and personality style will bring the best out of you to get the results you want. For more information email us at E: jen@jenharwood.com

Business Consulting

Our areas of specialisation include strategic planning, business plan development, marketing & sales, succession planning, business expansion and company documentation, including information memorandums and company profiles. Our team is highly qualified and trained in business and finance and most consulting projects are completed within 6-8 weeks. That's right, it's pretty quick. We don't have time to muck around – we get in, get to know you and all your staff, and get to work on planning, strategising and working the business strategies with you.

Our consulting style also factors in the non-core business issues the client is facing such as business partners, moving house, personal debt management, children, sick family members as well as other businesses the client may own and run. Some consulting projects qualify for 50% government assistance. We work with State & Federal funding programs to assist our clients apply for and secure funding assistance for projects. For more information email us at E: jen@jenharwood.com

Business Planning Programs

The Jen Harwood Pty Ltd Business Planning Program has seen over 140 companies from a variety of industries go through it in the last 2 years. The Program is all about getting business owners/managers clear on strategy and actually write a REAL business plan. Written and developed by Jennifer, this rigorous business program is conducted over 7 weeks where business owners receive both weekly workshops and business coaching to complete a comprehensive, relevant business plan.

Take note: This program is hard work, drives you nuts at times (as it makes you responsible for all your results – good and not so good) AND gives you results.. The program is run with 10 businesses at a time and really works. If you want this program in your area, email us at E: jen@jenharwood.com

BUSINESS PLANNNG PROGRAM QUOTES

"We got direction, confidence and motivation!"
Rosemary and Daryl Moait, Tyldwood Fine Foods

"Excellent, Enjoyable, Effective"
Derek Smith, Landlink Property Group

"I got greater balance for myself to manage both my business and family."
Kathie Bolitho, Bazzani Italiano

"I got a real sense of achievement from the goal setting and realisation process."
Jeff Williams, ParWill Swill

"I got control of business and my personal life BACK!"
Craig Dunn, Filthy Monkey Productions

"Everything good comes from Jen!"
Gerard Scott, Gerard Scott Homes

Who would you like to do business with?

Who can you help in your community with your network?

What value can you create, because you can?

OK dear reader, now it's up to you. You have new tools and strategies to be successful. DO something with them. Action creates results!

Go create and empower your networks! They are already waiting for you to show up...

Jennifer